Komi Can't Communicate

...akin to...
...?
...jeal-ousy.
...
STAAARE
SOME-ONE IS STARING AT ME ...

Communication 58: Emotional Pangs

UGGGHHHHH
...
GLOOM
...
...
STOP RIGHT THERE.
No running.
GRAB
GAH!
OH, UM... ONEMINE?
We're classmates.
Onemine is such a big sister.
HEY!

ARE YOU BUSY WITH CLASS COUNCIL, TADANO?
Why? Do you need me to do something too?
NO, NO! I CAME TO HELP!
Isn't that normal?
What do you want in return?
TADANO, I CAN TELL YOU'RE REALLY SUFFERING.
PEOPLE GIVE YOU TOO MUCH WORK!
You have to deliver these, huh?
NAJIMI, GET THE DOCS FROM THE PREP ROOM.
HA HA HA HA HA HA HA HA HA HA
TEE HEE! YOU'RE UNSTOPPABLE, ONEMINE!
NOW.
RIGHT.

FIDGET
FIDGET
Wants to help
KOMI, DO YOU WANT TO HELP TOO?
HM? IT'S NOT REALLY A THREE-PERSON JOB.
OH, RIGHT.
NEVER MIND, KOMI.
!
...
...

SO HOW'S SCHOOL TREATING YOU?
UH... WHY DO YOU ASK?
You sound like an aunt...
WELL ...
...YOU GET *TAKEN ADVANTAGE OF*, DON'T YOU?
TADOOOM
?!
NO, NOT REALLY ...
YOU DON'T ?
BUT I HEARD A TEACHER SAY, "AHH, I CAN LEAVE ALL MY WORK TO TADANO," WHILE SHE PLAYED MINESWEEPER ON HER COMPUTER.
Staff room
TAK TAK TAK
Ahh, can leave all my work to Tadano...
AGH! I DO GET TAKEN ADVANTAGE OF!

SO...
...IS THAT WHY YOU OFFERED TO HELP?
FUMP
BLUSH
OOPS! YOU CAUGHT ME!
I CAN'T STAND TO SEE SOMEONE SUFFER!
SHE'S SO NICE!
OH, ONE MORE THING.
IT'S ABOUT YOUR RELATIONSHIP WITH KOMI.
So nice!!
YES?
ARE YOU A MASOCHIST?
PINNNG
UM, WHY ARE YOU ASKING?

WELL, SHE'S BEAUTIFUL AND UNAPPROACHABLE, SO ISN'T SHE KIND OF *OVERBEARING*?
RRMMMMMMMM
Unh ?
OH... IS SHE?
BUT YOU'RE A NORMIE, SO— I MEAN, YOU'RE A REGULAR GUY, SO I THOUGHT...
...MAYBE YOU *ENJOY* HER HARSH GLARE.
SWEAT
SWEAT
BUT NEVER MIND! TO EACH HIS OWN!
YOU'VE GOT IT TOTALLY WRONG.
BESIDES, SHE ISN'T OVER-BEARING.
YOU SHOULD TRY TALKING TO HER.
IT'LL MAKE HER HAPPY! (AND TREMBLE.)
HMM... REALLY ?
BUT EVERYONE LOOKS UP TO HER...
...SO I BET SHE'S STUCK-UP.

NO, THAT'S NOT TRUE.
...!
OH ... ... OKAY.
ANYWAY, IF YOU NEED ANY HELP, JUST ASK ME!
SMAK SMAK
I'm full of energy!
TH- THANKS!
She's really nice!!
STAAARE
?!

HM? WHAT'S UP, KOMI?
JOLT
!!
...
STARE
!
YOU SHOULD TRY TALKING TO HER.
IT'LL MAKE HER HAPPY!
OH! HI THERE, KO–
SWIP
?!

WHAAAAAT?!
O
NO, YOU DON'T UNDER-STAND!
THERE'S AN EXPLA-NATION!
ACTUALLY... WHAT *IS* SHE DOING THERE?
After school
UGGGHHH
YOU GOT MORE WORK, HUH?
FINE. I'LL HELP YOU.
NO, YOU DON'T HAVE TO.
IF YOU REFUSE, THEN I'LL GIVE YOU EVEN MORE WORK!
One, two...
SO NICE!
Almost in tears

KOMI, YOU CAN GO HOME.
Don't wait for me!
!
...
...
...
NOD
All right, let's get this done!

SWUP
!
I want to help too.
HM?

S-SURE, ALL RIGHT. THANKS!
!
HMPH HMPH
Huh? Why is she so excited?
This sentence...
OHHHHH ...

OOPS! I FORGOT I HAVE SOME-THING TO DO!
I GOTTA GO! SORRY!
BYE, YOU TWO!
...
?
...
The next day
HI, YOU TWO!
!!

...
HM?
Sorry...
TOO CHUMMY?
Kyaah!
!
...!
SWUF SWUF
SWIP
I'm sorry for hiding when you spoke to me yesterday.
SWIP
!
!
SWUP
"Good morning."
BWA HA!
?!
AH HA HA! SORRY! THAT TICKLED MY FUNNY BONE!
?!
OH YEAH! HEY, KOMI?

Communication 58 — The End

DID YOU NOTICE THAT?

Komi Can't Communicate

SHWUF
10 October
1 2 3 4 5 6 7
Change uniform
8 9 10 11 12 13 14
16 17 18 19 20 21

HMPH
Checking one more time
...

BA-AAAM
KSHHHHHHHHHHHH
A MASSIVE TROPICAL CYCLONE IS APPROACHING HONSHU...
...AND A TYPHOON WARNING IS IN EFFECT!
KSHHHHHHHHHH

Communication 59: Typhoon

SHOKO, YOUR TEACHER JUST CALLED.
YOU'RE SUP-POSED TO STAY INDOORS FOR NOW.
!
No school ?!
...
...
Happy there's no school, but she changed uniforms and steeled herself to go, so now she feels a bit disappointed
...
GIRLS HER AGE ARE SO COMPLI-CATED...

KSHH HHHHHHH
Gets uneasy in inclement weather
JITTER JITTER
K IHHHHHHH
FWOO

SKWIK
SKWIK
HMPH
?!
FWASH

KA-BOOOOM
KYAH!
FWSH
OH? A POWER OUT-AGE?
ARE YOU OKAY, SHOKO?
Got fright-ened
THERE, THERE... COME TO MAMA.

RMBL
RMBL
RMBL
TRMBL
TRMBL
I'M GOING TO CHECK THE BREAKER. WAIT HERE.
!
FWASH
RUMMMBLE
JOLT
!!
Cell phone
?!!
JOLT

CALLING
Hitohito Tadano
!
BIP
UH, HELLO? KOMI?
ARE YOU STILL AT HOME?
...
YES.
GOOD. I WAS AFRAID YOU'D LEFT FOR SCHOOL.
I HEARD THERE'S A POWER OUTAGE IN YOUR NEIGHBORHOOD. ARE YOU ALL RIGHT?
UM ...
...YEAH. EVERY-THING'S FINE.
SERI-OUSLY? IT DOESN'T SOUND FINE...

KABOOM
BUMP
RATTLE
SHAKE
CLATTER
?!
K-KOMI! ARE YOU ALL RIGHT?!
...
KOMI?
I... I'M FINE.
THAT DIDN'T SOUND FINE!!
UM... UH...
YES?

CAN WE TALK ...
...A LITTLE LONGER ?
...!
YES, OF COURSE.

Communication 59 – The End

Communication 60: The Weather Clears

The Cat-Lovin' Princess
KOMI... WHY ARE YOU SO DREAMY?
YOU STIR MY HEART...
...IN YOUR BLUE MANTLE AND NIGHT-BLACK TIGHTS.
TADA A AH
*Only in her imagination
Komi
...
?!
BA M
OF COURSE I WANNA SEE YOUR PANTIES THROUGH THOSE TIGHTS!!
Fishing
SIGH... I NEED TO FIGURE OUT HOW TO SEE KOMI'S UNDERPANTS...
AH-HA!!
PINNNG
This can't end well...
KO-MI!
THERE'S A GIANT PUDDLE OUTSIDE! LET'S GO SEE!
A PUDDLE?
HMPH HMPH
THERE'S NO WAY THAT'LL-
YEP, SHE'S ON THE HOOK!

The Perfect Plan

Failure

Not Those

A Goddess Herself

Communication 60 — The End

Two days later...
I must see Komi's under-pants...
VEEEEEN
She looks so serious!!

Komi Can't Communicate

ONE DAY I WAS HUNGRY.
SO WHEN AFTERNOON CLASSES GOT CANCELED FOR A FIRE INSPECTION, I HURRIED OFF CAMPUS AND STRUCK OUT AT A BRISK PACE TOWARD THE STATION.
DON'T PANIC.
YOU'RE JUST HUNGRY.
BUT SO HUNGRY YOU COULD DIE!
WHY MUST I SUFFER SO?!
WHAT'RE YOU DOING?

Communication 61: Everyone Gets Gourmet

BING
BONG
BING
BONG
Yay! Only half a day of classes!!
KAPOOM
Let's go mess around!!
STUDYING ISN'T AN OPTION, HUH?
GRRRROWL
HEY!
AH HA HA! SOMEONE'S STOMACH IS GROWLING!
WHOSE IS IT?
OH.
GRRROWL
GROWWWL
GRUMLE
GRRROWL
GROWWWL
GRUMLE
GRRROWL
GROWWWL
GRUMLE
GRRROWL
GROWWWL
GRUMLE
?!

ITAN STREET
SWEAT
S-S-SORRY! M-MY S-STOMACH WON'T STOP GROWLING!
SWEAT
THANKS FOR INVITING ME TO GO EAT!!
IN RETURN, I'D LIKE TO...
...TAKE THIS OBBOR-
I M-MEAN, OPPORTUNITY...
She's too excited...
...TO HUMBLY RECOMMEND...
SWIP
...A NEARBY DINING ESTABLISHMENT.
?!
When it comes to food, Agari's a different person.
RECOMMEND ONE YOU'VE NEVER BEEN TO!
That'll be more fun!
?!

NITA DINER
TH-THIS IS THE ONLY RESTAURANT ON TH-THIS STREET ...
...THAT I'VE NEVER BEEN TO.
GLOOOOOM
IT LOOKS SORT OF RUN-DOWN ...
WHY HAVEN'T YOU BEEN?
IT'S ALWAYS EMPTY, SO I'D FEEL UNCOMFORTABLE ...
FIDGET
THAT'S UNDERSTANDABLE!
WHOOOSH
YA-HOO!
LET'S GO IN!!
WHASSUP?! SEATING FOR FOUR, PLEASE!!
NAJIMI IS A MONSTER OF UNRESTRAINT!

Moments before Komi and co. arrived ...
DAD ...
...
...THIS PLACE IS DE-SERTED.
...
Nita Diner Musubi Nita
Nita Diner Shinji Nita
BUT WHEN I SAID THERE WEREN'T ANY PATRONS FOR DINNER LAST NIGHT, YOU SAID THEY'D *THRONG* THE PLACE AT LUNCH!!
AW, SHADDUP! LET *ME* HANDLE THE BUSINESS SIDE OF THINGS! GO STUDY SO YOU AREN'T SUCH A DIM-WIT!!
I'M ONLY DUMB CUZ I TAKE AFTER *YOU!!*
HUH?! DON'T MOUTH OFF TO YOUR FATHER!! ONLY IDIOTS CALL OTHER PEOPLE IDIOTS!
WELL, YOU DID IT FIRST, YA DUMB DUMMY!
Father and daughter are a lot alike.
SIGH... I WISH A FAMOUS FOOD VIEWER WOULD COME...
WHAT'S A FOOD VIEWER?
A FOOD *REVIEWER*, DAD...
THERE'S A POP-ULAR FOOD CRITIC AROUND HERE ...
...WHO GOES BY *RAMEN-CORE.*
CLANG CLANG

Whassup?! Seating for four, please!!
WELCOME
CUSTOMERS?!
TUMP
UH... WEL-COME!
SIT ANY-WHERE YOU LIKE!
TUMP
...
HM?!
WHOA! W-W-WOW!
SPARKLE
SPARKLE
WHAT THE?! WOW-ZERS!!
SPARKLE

DAD! THAT MUST BE HER! THAT MUST BE RAMEN-CORE!
RAMEN WHAT?
I NEVER UNDER-STAND YOU.
I JUST TOLD YOU!! THERE'S A SUPER-FAMOUS CRITIC WHO POSTS REVIEWS ON THE FOODIE WEBSITE GURUNABE! AND THE NEXT DAY CUSTOMERS LINE UP LIKE CRAZY!
GURUNABE
THAT'S HOW TOMITA'S PLACE DOWN THE STREET GOT SO POPULAR!
Tomita (58)
GAH! SO THAT'S WHY!!
FROM WHAT I HEAR, RAMEN-CORE IS...
Ms. A
SHE'S A HIGH SCHOOL STUDENT!
SHE'S GOT AN AURA!
Mr. C
SHE'S PRETTY! With breasts like [redacted]!
Mr. B
AND LOVELY BLACK HAIR!
Mr. D
GLANCE
...
THAT'S HER!! THIS IS OUR MOMENT TO SHINE!!
The Nitas crave suc-cess.

WEL-COME! HERE'S YOUR WATER!
OH, THANKS.
TUNK
AND HERE'S YOUR WATER!
TUNK
?!
WHEN YOU'RE READY TO ORDER, JUST–
UM, EXCUSE ME.
WHERE'S OUR WATER?
OH ...
...I DIDN'T NOTICE YOU.
SHE DIDN'T NOTICE US?!

THEY'VE GOT QUITE A MENU!
I'M READY! HOW ABOUT YOU GUYS?
...
...!
TREMMMBLE
Can never decide in restaurants
TAKE YOUR TIME, KOMI. THERE'S NO HURR–
Yo! Order please!
ARGH!!

Ordering
I'LL HAVE THE FRIED OYSTERS!
CURRY, PLEASE.
Well, that's normal!
Shut up!
AND I...
...WILL HAVE YOUR NUMBER ONE SPECIALTY.
I SPEAK CLEARLY, WITHOUT A TRACE OF TIMIDITY, SO I WON'T HAVE TO REPEAT MYSELF.
...
WE DON'T GOT NO SPECIALTIES.
I'LL PUT YOU DOWN FOR NOTHING.
?!

?!
?!
Also wanted to order the specialty
How about this, miss? The deep-fried Itan chicken meal with goo-or-met grated radish!
It's our specialty!
SO THERE IS A SPECIAL-TY!!
PLEASE, WAIT A MOMENT.
Also got to order the specialty
...
GOO-OR-MET... GOURMET ?!
Tadano was at a loss for words ...

THANK YOU FOR WAIT-ING!
Miso soup with tofu (and seaweed)
Water
Cucumber pickles (well-pickled)
Rice (large)
Deep-fried chicken (six large pieces with plentiful shredded cabbage)
It looks deli-cious!!
HMPH HMPH
UM, WHERE'S OURS?
OOPS, I FOR-GOT!
COMIN' RIGHT UP!
SHE FORGOT! SHE FORGOT ABOUT US!!
GO AHEAD AND EAT.
It'll get cold.
!

MUNCH
CHEW CHEW
GULP

NCH CHEW MUNCH CHEW MUNCH CHEW MUNCH CH
!
!

AH, YES...
I FORGOT SOMETHING IMPOR-TANT.
WHEN THAT WOMAN WAS STILL HERE, THE DINER FLOUR-ISHED.
BUT I WAS SO BUSY THAT A GULF OPENED BETWEEN US.
AFTER SHE LEFT, I BLAMED THE CUSTOMERS.
I STOPPED COOKING FOR THEIR PLEASURE.
SO IT'S ONLY NATURAL THEY ABANDONED ME!
BUT TODAY, I COOKED AS HARD AS I COULD AND IT MADE ME REMEMBER SOMETHING.
I STARTED COOKING SO I COULD SEE PEOPLE'S SMILES !!
SWOOOOSH
WAS CHINESE STIR-FRY ON THE MENU?

THANKS FOR THE MEAL!!
EMPTY
THAT WAS DELICIOUS, WASN'T IT?
Yeah!
BUT THEY SERVED ME STIR-FRY...
CHEF NITA ...
!
...I EVALUATE YOUR SKILLS ...
...MOST HIGHLY.
!!

Communication 61 – The End

Komi Can't Communicate

Communication 62: Culture Festival Project

Komi Can't Communicate

GWOO
1-1
Class 1-1
The class was facing an unprecedented crisis.
The tension had reached a breaking point.
Insults and accusations flew.
Enter the mysterious group of delinquents that appeared in volume 1, communication 17!!!
BOY
Because the class was engaged in...

KOMI!
Komi!
...deciding its project for the culture festival!!
Komi!
Komi!
I WANT KOMI TO...
Komi!
Komi!
EVERYONE JUST CALM DOWN...
RICEBALLS
WHACK-A-
CAFE
BILLIARDS
CREP
MOVIE THEATER
HAUNTED HOUSE
FRANKFURTERS
Komi!
I WANT KOMI TO...
I WANT KOMI TO...
Komi!
Komi!
KOMI!
?!

Okay, that's enough!
Stop for a sec!
BAM
We took a vote and it was evenly divided!
So we'll hear the proposals again and take another vote!
And that's final! No grumbling about it!
THAT'S WHAT YOU WANTED TO SAY, RIGHT?
HUH?
UH, SURE. SOUNDS GOOD.
Awesome job, Tadano!

Najimi Osana's proposal
I STRONGLY RECOMMEND A MAID CAFE!
YOU MAY CONSIDER THAT...
...CLICHE AND OLD-FASHIONED...
...BUT ...
... wouldn't you like to see Komi in a maid outfit?
SNAPPPPP
HUH? YEAH, WE WOULD !!
?!

Ren Yamai's proposal
I THINK ...
...WE SHOULD DO A HAUNTED HOUSE!
WE CAN MAKE PROPS, DARKEN A CLASSROOM AND DEVISE A ROUTE.
IT WOULD BE HARD WORK AND COST A LOT OF MONEY...
... BUT THE EFFORT WOULD BUILD CAMARADERIE!
SCARY!
INSIDE
AND I COULD TOUCH KOMI'S BEHIND IN THE DARK!
PERK
M-MAYBE TRUE, BUT ...
?!

WHAT ABOUT YOU, NAKANAKA?
HUH?! ME?!
Omoharu Nakanaka's proposal
WE SHOULD FORM A ROCK BAND.
WE DON'T HAVE MANY OUTSTANDING MUSICIANS...
...SO MANY OF US WOULD LABOR OUTSIDE THE SPOTLIGHT.
BUT...
...WOULDN'T YOU LIKE TO HEAR KOMI SING?
MWA HA HA
OH, DEFINITELY!!
?!

Himiko Agari's proposal
Y-YOU WANT M-MY IDEA?!
I THINK *WHACK-A-MOLE* WOULD BE FUN!!
I WANT KOMI TO BONK ME!
Hit me as hard as you can!
BONK
IT'S GENIUS!!
?!
Class masochists
Mono Shinobino's proposal
WE SHOULD MAKE OUR OWN *MOVIE!*
A HISTORICAL DRAMA ABOUT RESCUING PRINCESS KOMI AFTER A BAND OF SHINOBI ABDUCT HER FROM HER VILLAGE! TEN MINUTES OF ACTION WOULD LEAVE EVERYONE SATISFIED!
A EUROPEAN SETTING WOULD BE COOLER!
YEAH! NONE OF THAT NINJA NONSENSE!
WE DON'T HAVE THAT KIND OF BUDGET...
Secret Komi Security

Nene Onemine's proposal
WE SHOULD SELL *RICE BALLS!*
EVERY-ONE WILL WANT SNACKS, RIGHT?
I'M GOOD AT MAKING RICE BALLS, SO–
KOMI'S RICE BALLS...
TOUCHED BY KOMI'S HANDS!!
HM?
...
Makeru Yadano's proposal
...
SOME-THING LIKE BOWLING OR BILLIARDS. ANYTHING WITH *WINNERS* AND *LOSERS!!*
GASP! MAKERU'S SO COOL!
MAKERU HAS A FAN CLUB?!
Makeru's fan club

Akako Onigashima's proposal
LET'S TELL LOVE FORTUNES!
LIKE WHO'S A GOOD MATCH FOR KOMI!
OOH! WE'D LIKE TO KNOW! ♡
Yuji Otaku's proposal
WE SHOULD SELL OUR OWN MANGA.
IF KOMI IS COSPLAYING AS A SALES GIRL, WE'LL MAKE A FORTUNE!
A NEW CHARACTER?!
Otaku isn't an otaku.
Ren Yamai's second proposal
MAYBE WE SHOULD SELL FRANKFURTERS!
STILL NEED KOMI TO EAT MY—
DON'T SAY IT!
BOOM BAP BAP
DA-BAROOM—
Nokoko Inaka's proposal
WE SHOULD HAVE A DISCOTHEQUE!!
SAY IT OUT LOUD!!

CAFE
HAUNTED HOUSE
WHACK-A-MOLE
RICEBALLS
BOWLING
BILLIARDS
DARTS
LOVE FORTUNES
It was an all-way tie.
I'M TELLING YOU! KOMI SHOULD...
Komi...
GRAAH
Komi!
KOMI AND I SHOULD...
Komi!
HISTORY REPEATS ITSELF...
Komi...
Komiii!
GRAAH
?!
Komi!
?!
Komi!
...
Komi!
UM, KOMI? WHAT DID YOU VOTE FOR?
Komi...
GRAAH
!
Komi...
Komi...

GRAAH
...
GRAAH
GRAAH
...
IT'S ALL RIGHT IF YOU'D RATHER NOT SAY.
!
GRAAH
GRAAH
...

SWUP
The maid cafe.

Communication 62 — The End

Communication 63: Accompaniment

?!
...?
...??
...
GLANCE
...
SWUF
SWUF
?!
WHAT'S WRONG?
Reason she couldn't ask: He's a boy.

AH HA HA
...
GWOOO
WHOA!
YOU STARTLED ME!
WHAT'S UP, KOMI?
...
GASP
...
?
?
Reason she couldn't ask: Which bathroom does Najimi use?

Reason she couldn't ask: She sensed it could be dangerous.
...
!

Communication 63 – The End

Komi Can't Communicate
Communication 64: Culture Festival Prep

Komi Can't Communicate

YAHOO
YAHOO
CHATTER
CHATTER
LIVELY
LIVELY

Maid Cafe
IF ANYONE ISN'T BUSY, I NEED HELP!
SOME-ONE THROW THIS OUT!
MOVE THOSE DESKS SO WE CAN BRING THIS IN!
FIDGET
FIDGET
Wants to help but can't
...

SOME-ONE HOLD THE OTHER END!
!
...
Some-one help!
...!
HMPH
SWOO
OH, UM, NEVER MIND! I'LL HANDLE IT!
!
KOMI, YOU CAN REST ON GOD'S THRONE!
God
BWAAAAAH
?!

God
Still wants to help
?!
?!
WE DON'T HAVE ENOUGH SUP-PLIES!
WE DON'T EITHER!
I NEED SOMEONE FROM THE FESTIVAL COMMIT-TEE!
Otori is super laid-back.
YEEEES?
WHAT DO YOU NEEEED?
WE NEED SOMEONE TO GO BUY MATE-RIALS.
...
SHUMP
OH, UH-HUUUUH.

...
SO... SEND SOME- ONE.
PWAAAAH
OHHH, UH- HUUUUH ...
IS SHE ALL RIGHT ?
SHALL I GO DO IIIIIIIT?
PWAH
HUH? ALL BY YOUR- SELF ?!
MAYBE... YOU SHOULDN'T GO ALONE.
OKAY. THEEEEEN ...
PWAH
PWAAAAH
KOMI, WOULD YOU LIKE TO COOOOOME ?
God
!!
?!

NO, UM, KOMI MUSTN'T ...
MURMUR
She's God!
Can we make her work?
BUT SHE ISN'T BUUUUSY. SO YOU CAN COME, RIIIIGHT?
MURMUR
God
...
Wants to help with the festival
God
Nervous about shopping with a classmate she doesn't know very well
...
God
TREMMMBLE
NOD
I'M WORRIED ABOUT THIS!
T

I'M WORRIED, SO I'LL GO WITH YOU.
THANKS, ONEMINE!
HEY, NO FAIR!
Onemine is such a big sister.
I'LL G-GO TOO!
OOH! ME TOO!
AND ME !!
BUT WE HAVE TO WORK HARD TO MAKE THE FESTIVAL A SUCCESS FOR KOMI ...
No, I better not...
SO THERE ISN'T A MOMENT TO LOSE!
Me nei-ther ...
DO IT FOR KOMI!
Or me...
?!
Con-fused
?!
Huh? Shop-ping?! I should go—
GLOMP
OH NO YOU'RE NOT!!
No skipping out on work!

The three girls went.
...
Hm? Are you nervous, Komi?
...!
We don't hang out much, huh?
Is this awkward?
...
Well, don't force yourself to talk.
Just take it easy ... okay? ...
...!
SHLUF
SHLUF
?!

CALM'S
HOME CENTER
WE'RE FINALLY HERE! It seemed to take forever...
SO? WHAT DO WE NEED?
BOARDS, PAINT, CLOTH... MM-HMM ...
ALL RIGHT! LET'S SPLIT UP!
...
NO, LET'S STAY TOGETH-ER.
AH HA HA
Onemine realized it might not be wise to leave the other two alone.

HOME CENTERS GET ME EXCITED!
HMPH HMPH
...!
OH, YOU AGREE?
OTORI, WILL THESE BOARDS WORK?
YES... I AGREEE.
BUT IT'S MY FIRST TIME HEEEERE.
HUH??
OH, YOU AGREE ABOUT GETTING EXCITED?
YOU'VE NEVER BEEN HERE, SO—
WHERE'D SHE GO?!
VANISHED
?!

SHE CAN'T BE FAR !!
TH- THIS IS AN EMERGENCY! LET'S SPLIT UP AND SEARCH!
NOD NOD
!
Staff only
CREAK
WHERE DID EVERYBODY GOOO?
NO ENTRY
?!
OHHHH ...
...HOW ARE YOU DOING, KOOOOMI ?
...
TUG

WERE YOU LOOKING FOR ME? SOOOOORRY.
...
ARE YOU ANGRYYYYY ?
!
...!!
SWUF SWUF
OHHHHH ...
PWAAAG
...WHAT A RE-LIEEEEEF.
...
...
SMIIILE
...

...
IT SEEMS LIIIIKE ...
FIDGET
FIDGET
...YOU WANT TO SAY SOME-THIIIIING.
!
BUT THERE'S NO HUUURRY.
PWAH
I'M SUUUU-PER LAID-BACK...
...SO IF YOU TAKE YOUR TIIIIIME ...
...!
... THAT'S FINE WITH MEEEE.
FWIP
FWIP
...
Writing on the floor
SKRK SKRK SKRK SKRK SKRK
OHHHHH, YOU TALK BY WRITING?

Why did you invite me?
HMM... GOOOOOOD QUESTION.
PWAAH
I DON'T ACTUALLY KNOOOOOW.
?!
BUT...
... WHEN I SEE YOU WITH TADANO AND NAJIMI ...
...I WAAANT ...
...TO BE YOUR FRIEND TOOOOO.
!
SKRK SKRK
In junior high
I couldn't help much with class events, so I didn't join in often.

In junior high
I couldn't help much with class events, so I didn't join in often.
I wish I had helped more.
I wish I had helped more.
So today when you invited me
me
join in often
I was happy.
?!
VANISHED
HEY, KOMI?
WHAT'S THIIIIS THING?
VRRRR
No, miss!
?!

THERE YOU ARE! I HEARD A NOISE! ARE YOU ALL RIGHT?
!
HI, ONE-MIIIIIINE.
DON'T GET INTO TROUBLE, OKAY?
They finished.
ONEMINE, KOMI AND I ARE FRIENDS NOOOOW.
OH, THAT'S NICE.
BUT YOU'RE MY FRIEND TOOOOO.
UH... THANKS.
TEE-HEEEEEE ...
...
HEY, KOOOOOMI ?

LET'S WORK HARD FOR THE FESTIVAL, OKAAAAAY?
Okay.

Communication 64 — The End

THE DOUBLE-O DUO!!
BOTH LAST NAMES START WITH O!!
ONEMINE
OTORI
WHY ARE YOU TELLING US THAT?
EASY TO DRAW

Komi Can't Communicate

Komi Can't Communicate

Communication 65: Distributing Flyers

SUNFLOWER
SHOW US HOW.
To hand out the flyers.
WELL, IF I HAVE TO!
Hey, guy! Put this up, will ya?!
DASH
THAT WAS FAST!!
THEY'RE STILL TALKING...
He said he'll do it!
AND HE GAVE ME SOME CRO-QUETTES!
So eat up!
NAJIMI'S THE VERY INCARNATION OF SOCIA-BILITY!

I think I can do it.
HMPH HMPH
R-REALLY?
THEN LET'S GET CRACKING!
TOMITA
color type
...
WANDER
WANDER
WANDER
TOMITA
color type
...
GLANCE
...
IS SHE ALL RIGHT?
TOMITA
color type

!
AH HA HA HA
GWO
?!
OOOOO GAH
UM... WELCOME ?
WHY IS SHE JUST STARING? But she sure is pretty!
RATTLE
!
...!
...!!
UM, COME ON IN!
...!!

WHAT WOULD YOU LIKE?
Komi sat down.
TREMMMBLE
!!
...
...!
...!!
...!!!
HM?
I KNOW!! SHE'S SO HUNGRY SHE CAN BARELY SPEAK !!
?!
WELL THEN! I'LL MAKE SOMETHING TO FILL HER UP!
TADUMMM
?!
Just ate and came back
SHAME
TOMITA
SHAME
SERI-OUSLY ?!

UM, LET'S TRY A PLACE YOU'RE FAMILIAR WITH.
I handed out some more!
!
BEYOUGH SHEETS
HM?
SHOKO?
ARE THESE YOUR FRIENDS?
Hiya!
NOD

THE RUMORS WERE ABOUT YOU, HUH?
RUMORS?
ANYWAY, HOW CAN I HELP YOU?
!
...
...
...!
...?!
OH, YOU WANT ME TO DISPLAY A FLYER.
YOU'VE BEEN COMING HERE FOR FOUR YEARS, KOMI?
...
...
Oh...
Uh-huh...
HE CAN TALK TO HER!!
Does he have super powers like Karisu?!
WHOAA!

RAMEN RIGHT?!
NOD
TREMMBLE
A sympathetic resonance between sufferers of communication disorders

NITA DINER
TEL 012-3456
NITA DINER
HI THERE!
IT'S THAT POPULAR REVIEWER AGAIN!!
*The Nitas believe Komi is a popular online reviewer.
WE OWE HER MAJOR RESPECT !!
BOW
HM? FLYERS ?
PLASTER 'EM OVER THE WHOLE SHOP!!
TADAAAAAH
They smothered the diner.

WE'VE GOT ONE FLYER LEFT! LET'S HIT UP THIS HOUSE!
DING DONG
WHY DON'T YOU *EVER* HESITATE?
YES? WHO IS IT?
WAAAAH
!
SORRY, MA'AM. DID WE WAKE THE BABY?
NAH, HE'S ALWAYS LIKE THIS!
WAAAAH
ALWAYS?
WE'RE STUDENTS FROM ITAN HIGH SCHOOL. WE'RE HAVING A CULTURE FESTIVAL AND...
BWAAAAH
WAAAAH
SORRY...
...THIS IS THE FLYER, SO...

ANYWAY, WE HOPE YOU'LL COME SEE IT.
GWOOO
BWAAAAH
GWOOOOOO
BW-
—
—
SMILE
THE BABY STOPPED CRYING.
AH HA HA
FWIP
?
KO-KO!
KO-KO!
WHAT'S GOTTEN INTO YOU?

Communication 65 — The End

Communication 66: Culture Festival Eve

HI, BOYS! WE MADE RICE BALLS!
But those words bring the corpses back to life!
BWAAAAH
CHATTER CHATTER
WAIT... DID KOMI MAKE SOME OF THESE?!
WHICH ONES?! URGH... I DON'T KNOW!!
CHATTER
CHATTER
Small rice balls
Strangely shaped rice balls
Big rice balls
Perfect rice balls
WHO MADE WHICH RICE BALLS?!!

Najimi's statement
I MADE RICE BALLS WITH STRANGE SHAPES!
Like squares and rhombuses!
Onemine's statement
MINE WERE A LITTLE BIG.
But I'm sure you can finish them!
Komi's statement
KOMI'S ARE PERFECTLY FORMED!
...
Yamai's statement
KOMI MADE SMALL ONES!! AND THEY AREN'T PERFECT!!
SO LEAVE THE PERFECT ONES TO ME!!
One of these people is lying. Guess which one!

In the end, they decided by rock-paper-scissors.
ONE... TWO...
I'll save this rice ball forever!!
I'll put mine on the home altar!
What a trea-sure!
DID I GET NAJIMI'S?
BUT IT SURE IS A PERFECT CUBE!
How could anyone make this?
MUNCH MUNCH
!
HEY, THIS IS GOOD!

Communication 66 – The End

KOMI COPIED NAJIMI AND MADE ONE RICE BALL IN A STRANGE SHAPE.
WHAT A PERFECT CUBE, KOMI!

Komi Can't Communicate

CHATTER CHATTER
WOOOO
WEL-COME TO THE 23RD...
...ITAN HIGH SCHOOL CULTURE FESTI-VAL!!
ITAN FESTIVAL
A.K.A. KOMI FEST!
1-1 MAID CAFE ITAN

?!
?!
?!
HM?
WHAT'S WRONG, KOMI?
SWIP SWIP
POINK POINK
OH, DID YOU WANT A LONG SKIRT?
?!
AH HA HA! AIN'T HAPPENIN'!
Yamai col-lapsed!!
Did she faint?!
JUST KIDDING! WE MADE A LONG ONE FOR YOU!
BUT WHY NOT STICK WITH A SHORT ONE?!
MAID CHANGING ROOM
!!
SWUF SWUF
She didn't faint!!
She's taking a video from a low angle!!
WHAT A NOISY GROUP ...

Communication 67: Maids

MAGIC SHOW
GUERRILLA THEATER
The maid cafe expert rises early.
祭
Maid Cafe Expert Tatsuhito Akido (32)
He wakes at 6 a.m. and checks for new maid cafe openings.
After a light breakfast, he decides which cafe he will visit.
He visits one per day.
And he gives that decision his total concen-tration.
After deciding, he cleanses himself ...
...so as not to offend the maids with poor personal hygiene.
As their master, he must comport himself like a gentleman...
MAID CAFE ITAN
Today, he has chosen to visit the Itan High School culture festival...
...and Class 1-1's maid cafe!!

It's just a high school culture festival, so his expectations aren't high.
Want some home-made cookies?
3-2 INDIE FILM
But if the quality is dreadfully low, he is prepared to issue a stern—
Wel-come home, Master!
OH, UH... THANKS...
BLUSH
BLUSH
Akido is your average nerd, so he gets flustered around flesh-and-blood girls.
Please, wait a moment.
Um, okay.
FOR A MERE SCHOOL FESTIVAL, THIS ISN'T BAD...
But in his head, he adopts a superior attitude.

The time of darkness approaches ...
...so choose your poison!
HMM... SHE'S OBVIOUSLY GOING THROUGH A PHASE ...
Whoops!
Sh-shorry about that!
SPLAAAT
YES... THE BUSTY KLUTZ IS INDISPENS-ABLE...
HURRY UP ALREADY.
SLAM
AHH... I DO LIKE THE SURLY TYPE...
THEY HAVE A FINE LINEUP, BUT—
TREMM
MMMBLE
?!

TREMMMBLE
UM ...
WHAH ?!
UH ...
GOOD JOB AT WORK TODAY, MAS-TER!
WHAT WOULD YOU LIKE FOR DINNER ?
HUH?! UM...
I'LL HAVE THE MAIDENLY LOVE RICE OMELET.
As you wish !
BABINNNG
AND THAT ONE'S ENERGETIC. VERY AGREE-ABLE, BUT...
...
TREMMMMMMBLE
WH-WHO IS SHE?!

GWOOOOOO
W-WHY IS SHE GLARING AT ME?
GASP!!
IT MUST BE BECAUSE I'VE BEEN DIS-COURTEOUSLY APPRAISING THE MAIDS HERE...
INDEED, IT IS WRONG TO LUST AFTER THE HELP!
!!
IS THAT WHY SHE'S ANGRY?
KLINK
S...
...r...
...so...
SWOOO
I'M SO R... RIGHT?! I KNEW IT!!
She tried to say, "I'm sorry."

HERE'S YOUR RICE OMELET!
MUTTER
Th...
MUTTER
Thank you...!!
WRITE "MAID CAFE ITAN ❤" WITH THE KETCHUP!
MUTTER
I've visited too many maid cafes...
MUTTER
...and forgotten what's impor-tant.
...
...!!
Got nervous and messed up
MUTTER
One's relation-ship with a maid ...
MUTTER
... must always be platonic !!
MUTTER
CAN YOU EVER FORGIVE M-
AN X?! DOES THAT MEAN NO?!

I'LL BE GOING NOW.
Finished eating
!
GLOOOM
Thinks he's depressed because of her poor service
GLOOOM
...
COME AGAIN ...
...!
!

Communication 67 – The End

Communication 68: Tadano's a Maid Too

Tadano
WHAT'RE YOU DOING, TADANO?!
He doesn't look bad...
YOU LOOK AWFUL, TADANO!
Actu-ally, he looks pretty good!
1-1 MAID CAFE ITAN
SERI-OUSLY. SHUT UP
STAAARE
HMPH HMPH
HMPH
HMPH
CAN I TAKE THIS OFF NOW?!
HUH? I THOUGHT YOU WERE *COMMIT-TED* TO THIS.
NO, YOU *FORCED* ME TO WEAR IT!

SHOKO! I CAME!
KOMI'S MOM IS HERE!
RIGHT THIS WAY, MA'AM!
YOU LOOK GOOD, SHOKO!
THANK YOU!
H- HERE'S YOUR WATER.
HM? TADANO?
UH, YEAH.
OHHH...
...I UNDERSTAND.
NO, DON'T GET THE WRONG IDEA!

COME ON, SHOSUKE! WHAT'S TAKING SO LONG?!
SHO ...
... SUKE ?
WHOAAA!! H-HE'S COOL! AND CUUUU-ÙÙUUU-ÚÚTE!
BABU
MP
And a host of maids gathered ...
God
?!
DADUMMM
KYAAAH
Shosuke felt uncom-fortable, so he left immediately.

HEY, BRO! I HAD SOME FREE TIME, SO I CAME TO CHECK IT OUT!
!
UMMM...
DON'T REACT LIKE THAT!
Pony Ericsson
CLICK
HI, MOM? DID YOU SEE THAT? YEAH.
HE REALLY IS LIKE THAT.
LIKE THAT?! LIKE WHAT?!

MAIDS ON BREAK
1-1 MAID CAFE
GOOD WORK, KOMI.
!
...
GLANCE
...
GOOD THING IT'S A SUCCESS, HUH?
!!
GLANCE
GLANCE
...!!
NOD NOD
BUT I LOOK RIDICULOUS, RIGHT? *RIGHT*?
!!!
...!!!
SHAKE SHAKE

Communication 68 – The End

Hitomi Tadano Isn't Ordinary!! Part ①

Komi Can't Communicate

Komi Can't Communicate

Communication 69: Najimi's Maid Cafe

Hello! Welcome home, Master!
BAM
We're cheap, cheap, cheap!!
Pardon me, Master! We've got good maids!
Wanna come in for a drink? Huh? Well do ya?! Thanks!
I've got discount tickets! Dally with our top-quality maids! Spe-cial options available!
1-5
WARABIMOCHI
HORRIBLE HAUNTED HOUSE
Hey, boy! Want a maid souvenir?
The cover charge is one grand! Free charm included!
HUSTLE
It's hot out! But we've got chilled towels!
BUSTLE
WHY IS NAJIMI SUCH A PRO AT THIS?!

CHATTER
CHATTER
CHATTER
CHATTER
...
I CAN DO MORE ...
LIKE WHAT?!
KOMI! TAKE A STROLL FOR 100 METERS AROUND THE CAFE!
CHATTER
CHATTER
FWOOSH
!
CHATTER
CHATTER
OUT

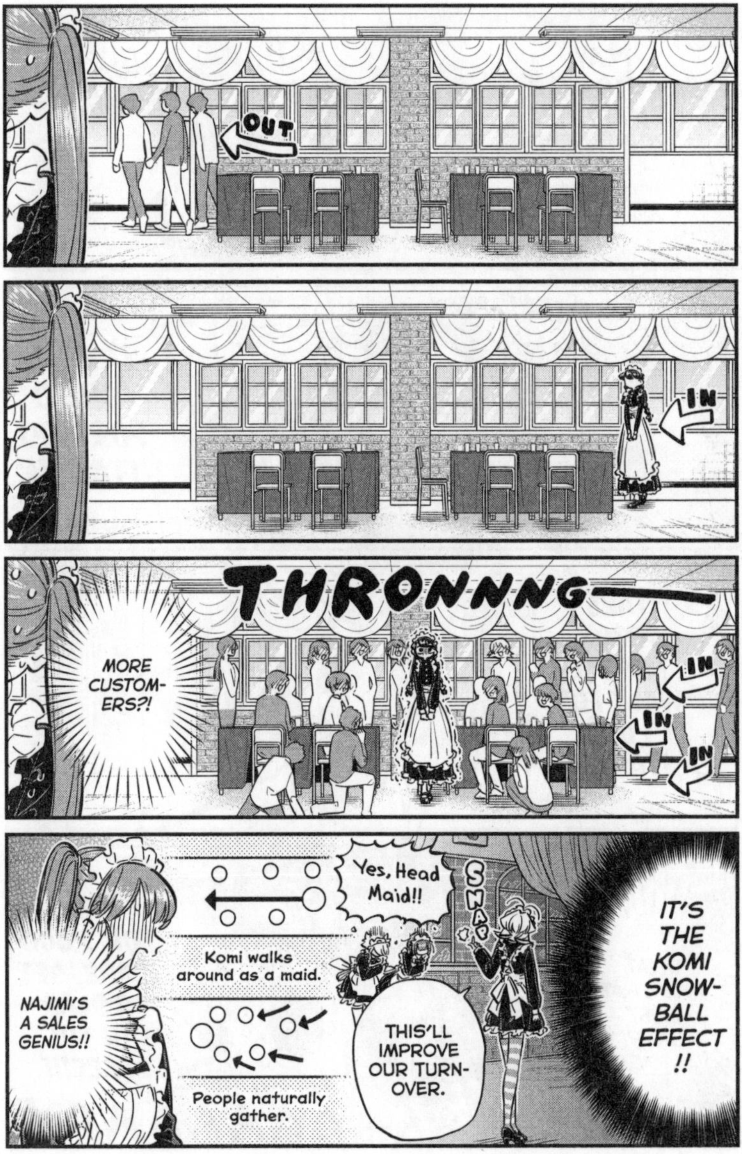

OUT
IN
THRONNNG—
IN
IN
IN
MORE CUSTOMERS?!
IT'S THE KOMI SNOWBALL EFFECT!!
SNAP
THIS'LL IMPROVE OUR TURNOVER.
Yes, Head Maid!!
Komi walks around as a maid.
People naturally gather.
NAJIMI'S A SALES GENIUS!!

PLAY GAMES WITH A MAID FOR 300 ITANS!
*Itan: unit of currency at the Itan High School Culture Festival.
LOOK THATAWAY...
...HEY!
TAKE A PHOTO FOR 500 ITANS!!
MAID CAFE ITAN
TAKE A 30-MINUTE WALK FOR 1,000 ITANS!!!
AND! FOR 2,000 ITANS, GET A SLAP IN THE FACE!!!
WHAT WAS THAT LAST ONE?!
YAAAAAAAAAAAAAAY

Communication 69 — The End

Komi Can't Communicate

Communication 70: Culture Festival, Part 1

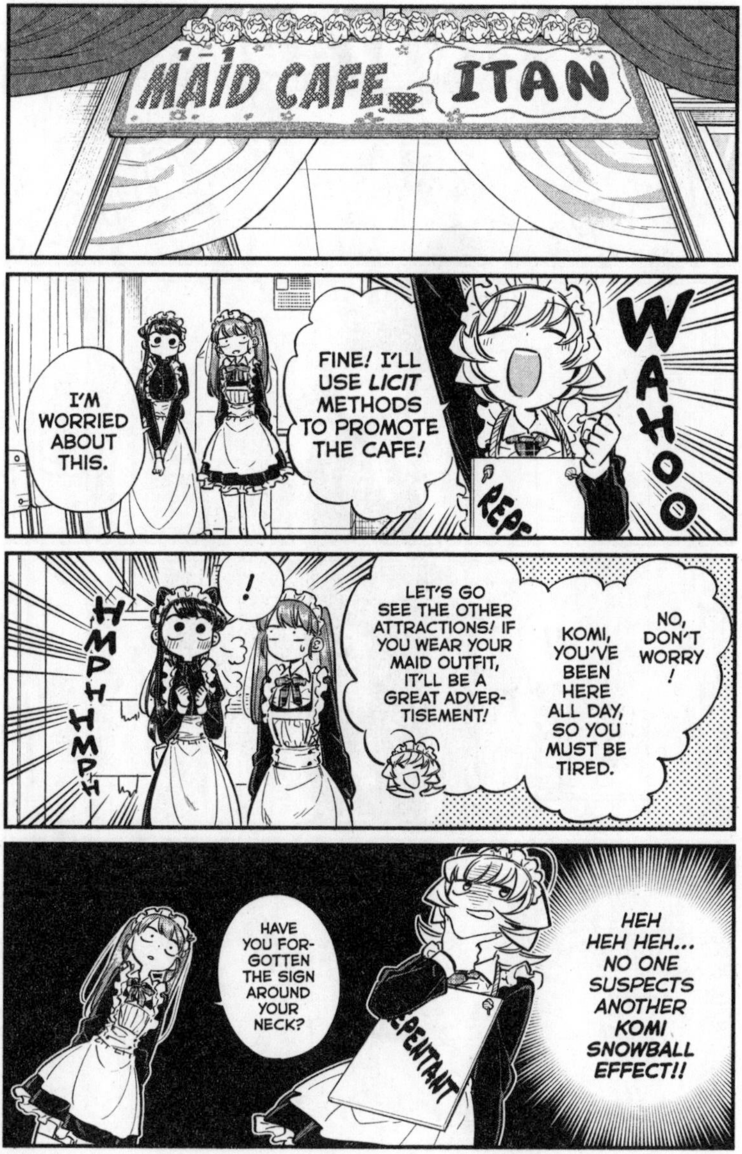
1-1 MAID CAFE ITAN
WAHOO
FINE! I'LL USE *LICIT* METHODS TO PROMOTE THE CAFE!
I'M WORRIED ABOUT THIS.
NO, DON'T WORRY!
KOMI, YOU'VE BEEN HERE ALL DAY, SO YOU MUST BE TIRED.
LET'S GO SEE THE OTHER ATTRACTIONS! IF YOU WEAR YOUR MAID OUTFIT, IT'LL BE A GREAT ADVERTISEMENT!
!
HMPH HMPH HMPH
HEH HEH HEH... NO ONE SUSPECTS ANOTHER KOMI SNOWBALL EFFECT!!
HAVE YOU FORGOTTEN THE SIGN AROUND YOUR NECK?

IT AN FE ST IV AL
1-2 PLAY
MODERN
LITTLE RED
RIDING HOOD
STARTING TIMES
10:00~ 16:00~
12:00~
14:00~
CHATTER
CHATTER
3-3 CROSS-DRESSING BAR 3-3 IN CLASSROOM 3-3
!
!
1-2 PLAY MODERN LITTLE RED RIDING HOOD
!!
!!
SPIN SPIN
!!
!!
SPIN SPIN
THE KOMI DRILL !!

OH! A HAUNTED HOUSE! LET'S GO IN!
1-4 SCARY HAUNTED HOUSE
!
NOD NOD
Doesn't like scary stuff
IT'S PRETTY DARK IN HERE ...
...
WWOO
...!!
FLINCH
GRAAAH
BEWARE OF BEARS
...!!!
A bear?
FLINCH
Gelatin brick
SPLAT
...?!?! ?!?!?!
(A silent scream.)
...

?!
?!
?!
It's j-just gelatin.
HERE COMES SOME-BODY!
Scarer: Shizuka Odoka
THEY'RE ALMOST HERE...
GAH!! IS TH-THAT KOMI ?!
TREMMMBLE
W-WHAT SHOULD I DO?! KOMI IS A SYMBOL OF OUR SCHOOL! SHOULD I REALLY SCARE HER?!
I DON'T WANT HER TO HATE ME!!
BUT SCARING PEOPLE IS MY JOB!
BUT IF I'M NOT SCARY, KOMI WILL BE DISAP-POINTED !!
NO! I'M GONNA SCARE HER!! NOW! NOW!!
Komi already passed.

EXIT
EXIT
INDIE MOVIE SCREENING 3-2 CLASSROOM
WHACK-A-MOLE
TEDDY BEAR
Join me!
AH HA HA! THAT WAS FUN!!
HEY! THEY'RE DOING CONFESSIONS ON THE ROOF!!
LET'S GO SEE!
!
SW
WH
"Confessions on the roof?"
STUDENTS GO ON THE ROOF AND SHOUT SECRETS AND LOVE CONFESSIONS!
I'm in love with you!!
THANKS BUT NO THANKS!!
"I've never heard of that."
...
WANNA DO IT?
AGH! NAJIMI ALWAYS DOES THIS!!

Decided to watch it first
NEXT IS YAMAI FROM CLASS 1-1!
OH! THAT'S YAMAI!
TODAY, I'M GOING TO PROCLAIM MY LOVE FOR SOME-ONE!
WHO IS IT?!
I'M IN LOVE WITH KOMI IN CLASS 1-1!
HANG OUT WITH ME AND WE'LL GET MARRIED WHEN WE'RE OLDER!!
KYA
AAH
?!
...
TEE HEE! KOMI'S EMBARRASSED SPEECHLESS!!!
REPENTANT

NEXT IS KOMI, WHO BLEW OFF THE LAST CONFESSION WITH INESTIMABLE GRACE!
DO IT TO ADVERTISE THE MAID CAFE!
?!
?!
...
...
...
...
AAAAAAA
KOMI!!
A MAAAID!
WOOOO
?!

...
...
Me... ...ow!
Started to say "maid" but bit her lip
ME... OW?
MEOW... MEOW!
CHATTER
IS SHE A CAT?
A CAT MAID?!
CHATTER
KOMI'S A MAID WITH CAT EARS!!
WH-WHOA-AAAAA-AAAA!! THAT'S A MUST-SEE!!
About to faint from nerves
TEETER
WAAAAAAAAAH

AH HA HA HA! AWESOME ADVER-TISEMENT, KOMI!!
WHEW!
...!
...!!
OF TOP CON FES
HEY! DON'T USE KOMI LIKE THAT!
3-3 CROSS-DRESSING BAR 3-3 IN CLASSROOM 3-3
AH HA HA! EMBARRASSING MOMENTS ARE THE BEST PART OF CULTURE FESTIVALS!!
Are you a demon ?!
WAS IT FUN?

Communication 70 – The End

THWACK
GYOOOW
REPENTANT

Komi Can't Communicate

Communication 71: Culture Festival, Part 2

WHAT'S WRONG?
...
"People are looking at me more than usual."
!
THAT'S BECAUSE YOU LOOK ADORABLE AS A MAID.
!!

SQUIRM
FIDGET
...
BLUSHHH
...!
BLUSHHH
...!!
?
WHAMM
W-WHAT'S WRONG?
OW!!

TADANO, YOU CAN BE INCREDIBLY DENSE FOR SUCH A PERCEPTIVE PERSON.
HUH?
ANYWAY, WANNA CHECK OUT MORE ATTRACTIONS WITH US?
ASTRONOMY CLUB
!
NOD
"US"?
HM? KAEDE WAS RIGHT BEHIND ME, BUT ...
KAEDE? OH, SHE MEANS OTORI.
Kaede Otori
Can you find Otori in this panel?
FILM SCREENING
CREPES $2.00
CUPCAKES 1 FOR $1.00
PENGUIN YAKITORI

上映会
OH, THERE SHE IS!
HOW DID YOU SEE HER?!
T
Otori joined them.
THERE'S SOOOOO MUCH ...
...INTER-ESTING STUUUUFF HERE.
MANGA CLUB LAST $3.00
MANGA CLUB
MANGA

FLIK
RUNNING AWAY
TIME LEFT:
3:12
PRIZE: ICE CREAM
ART CLUB✦
CARICATURES
RRRRRIP
IT'S NO USE!! YOU'RE BEYOND MY SKILLS!!
You're too gorgeous!!
?!

THERE'S A BAND IN THE CENTRAL PLAAAAZA.
GREAT! LET'S GO SEE!
CHATTER
CHATTER
ITAN festival
CLANG
DOOOM
HEAVY METAL?
THADA
BOOM
IS KOMI ALL RIGHT WITH ALL THIS NOISE?
RATTLE
SHAKE

Communication 71 — The End

Communication 72: The After-Party

HOWEVER, A CERTAIN STUDENT (NAJIMI) USED INAPPROPRIATE PROFIT-MAKING SCHEMES...
HURRAAA-
1-1 MAID CAFE JAN
...SO THE PRIZE IS REVOKED!
...
SILENCE
BUT ...
...it was fun, right?
GRIN
DON'T TRY TO SPIN THIS!

AFTER WE WORKED SO HARD... TOO BAD, HUH?
!
But it was fun.
BABMP
HWAAAH?!!
Your reaction was totally differ- ent...
... when I said it!!!
AH HA HA
BUT THEY STILL WEAR SMILES!
WHAT A WON- DERFUL CLASS!
I score it 200 degrees!

NOW FOR A DANCE PARTY TO THE SWINGIN' SOUNDS OF THE SCHOOL BRASS BAND!
GET INTO THE GROOVE AND HAVE FUN!
AND DON'T FORGET TO EAT YOUR FILL AT THE BUFFET!
KOMI, LET'S DANCE!
??!
OOF!
WHSH WHSH
KOMI! DANCE WITH ME!
OOF!
SHALL WE DANCE?
SWSH
Komi!
Komi!
BIFF POW
?!
Komi!!
BAM THOK
?!
DON'T MIND THEM.

HMPH
HMPH
KOMI SEEMS EXCITED ...
Wants to dance
PWOINK
OH, NOW SHE'S CALM ...
But she's too embar-rassed.
GLANCE
WHY IS SHE LOOKING AT ME?

HM?
HUH?!
SHOULD I INVITE HER TO DANCE?
BUT...
...WE'D HAVE TO GET CLOSE...
...AND HOLD HANDS!!
BESIDES, I DOUBT SHE WANTS TO DANCE WITH ME...
...RIGHT?
AH HA HA! AH HA HA HA...
...
...
UM...

...WOULD YOU...
...LIKE TO DANCE?
...!
NOD

Komi?!
She's dancing!
Who's that other girl?
WIGGLE
Has no idea how to dance
WIGGLE
I'LL T-TRY HOLDING HANDS ...
S-SORRY ...

Communication 72 — The End

Komi Can't Communicate

Komi Can't Communicate

Grabbing Tadano's Boobs, Part 1

Komi Can't Communicate

Grabbing Tadano's Boobs, Part 2

There's no "Can Komi Make 100 Friends?" this time. I really wanted to do the boob story. I apologize from the bottom of my heart.

A Collaborative Manga with *Sleepy Princess*

Both titles are now available from VIZ Media!

Komi Can't Communicate X Sleepy Princess in the Demon Castle

Komi meets Princess Syalis!!

The *Shonen Sunday* heroines team up!!

Welcome to Bonus Communication: Sleepy Princess

Bonus Communication: Sleepy Princess

Freaking out because she doesn't know where she is
GLANCE GLANCE
...?!
...?!
...
...
Deciding to take a look around
HMPH
MURMUR MURMUR
Hm? Hey...
CHATTER CHATTER
Who's that?
A new princess?
FWISH
She's cute ...

Huh? Huuuh?
Say whaaaat?!
H...
Hey, you!
FLINCH
TREMMMMMMMMMMMMMMMMMMMMMMMMBLE
?!
?!
?!
Yahoo! She's scared of us!!
Totally not scared of them
SHAKE
SHAKE
SHAKE
SHAKE
HEAVE-HO
We can't just let her wander around.
We'll take her to the cells.
HEAVE-HO
HEAVE-HO
Dang. They're being cleaned ...
CHATTER
CHATTER
Let's stow her here for now.
CLANK
PEEK
!
STAAARE
?!

Bonus Communication: The End

Komi Can't Communicate

VOL. 5
Shonen Sunday Edition

Story and Art by Tomohito Oda

English Translation & Adaptation/John Werry
Touch-Up Art & Lettering/Eve Grandt
Design/Julian [JR] Robinson
Editor/Pancha Diaz

Original Cover Design/Masato ISHIZAWA + Bay Bridge Studio

Printed in Italy

Published by VIZ Media, LLC
P.O. Box 77010
San Francisco, CA 94107

10 9 8 7 6 5 4
First printing, February 2020
Fourth printing, March 2022

viz.com

shonensunday.com

PARENTAL ADVISORY
KOMI CAN'T COMMUNICATE is rated T for Teen and is recommended for ages 13 and up.

ratings.viz.com

Tomohito Oda won the grand prize for *World Worst One* in the 70th Shogakukan New Comic Artist Awards in 2012. Oda's series *Digicon*, about a tough high school girl who finds herself in control of an alien with plans for world domination, ran from 2014 to 2015. In 2015, *Komi Can't Communicate* debuted as a one-shot in *Weekly Shonen Sunday* and was picked up as a full series by the same magazine in 2016.

Kidnapped by the Demon King and imprisoned in his castle, Princess Syalis is...bored.

SLEEPY PRINCESS IN THE DEMON CASTLE

Story & Art by
KAGIJI KUMANOMATA

Captured princess Syalis decides to while away her hours in the Demon Castle by sleeping, but getting a good night's rest turns out to be a lot of work! She begins by fashioning a DIY pillow out of the fur of her Teddy Demon guards and an "air mattress" from the magical Shield of the Wind. Things go from bad to worse—for her captors—when some of Princess Syalis's schemes end in her untimely—if temporary—demise and she chooses the Forbidden Grimoire for her bedtime reading...

RATED T TEEN

VIZ

Komi Can't Communicate has been printed in the original Japanese format to preserve the orientation of the artwork.

Follow the action this way.